Stories from the Skylands
An Exciting Minecraft Novel for Kids!

~From the Minecraft Books For Kids Series~

By Brock Netherward

Table of Contents

Chapter 1: Meet Rozzie & Grayson

Rosella's house was warm, and it was dry, and it was comfortable. And yet, all she wanted to do was go outside. Even now, when the rain was hitting the glass of the window with a strong, rattling force. She had sat by the window on a high-backed wooden chair, and she watched the sun set through the curtain of pouring rain.

There was a fire burning in the fireplace. The warmth soaked through the wool blanket that she had wrapped herself in, and the smell of wood smoke made her sleepy. She looked over at the fireplace. Every once in a while, there would be a popping sound, or one of the logs would shift as they burned. She yawned, stretched, and threw her wool blanket onto the ground. She stood up and stretched again.

She walked over to the fireplace. Everyone in her family kept their shoes. She picked her boots up, sat back down, and started to pull them on. They had been warmed by the fire, and had mostly dried out since she had trekked through the swamp earlier in the day.

"Where are you going?" came her mother's voice. Rosella knew at that moment that she was in trouble. She had not even realized that her mother was in the room.

"Out," Rosella said. "I'll be back soon."

"It's raining, Rozzie," her mother said.

"I noticed. Be back soon", said Rosella. She finished putting on her boots and made a move to the door. If she could only get out before her mother had a chance to say anything, she would be in the clear. But her mother was too quick on the draw.

"It's not happening. Take those boots off and sit back down."

Rosella paused at the door. She thought about just walking out the door. It would not be the first time that she had just walked out. However, every time she had done that, she'd been grounded the moment she came home. Rosella was in no mood to get grounded. Plus, she thought, the trader is coming tomorrow. If I get grounded, I won't get to buy anything. The trader didn't come to the village often—usually once every two months, but less in the winter and more in the summer. Rosella had learned a long time ago that you had to be on your best behavior when something interesting was about to happen. The danger of being punished was just too great.

She turned around. "Please? I won't be out for long, I promise."

Her mother shook her head. "Sorry, Rozzie. Almost every piece of clothing you owned is soaked through with rain."

"Well it's been raining for days," Rosella said. She had been going crazy stuck inside the house for so long. It was not a big house, and she shared it with both her parents, as well as her younger sister Gloria. Even when she was alone in the house—which was rare—it felt cramped. "Just let me go out for a bit."

Her mother shook her head again. "Sorry, sweetie. Go get some sleep. Maybe the rain will be gone tomorrow."

Rosella sighed. What could she do? She pulled her boots back off, dropped them in front of the fire, and walked off to the bedroom that she shared with Gloria. Her sister was already sound asleep on the bottom bunk. Rosella climbed to the top bunk. She was restless, and it took her a long time to fall asleep.

After about forty-five minutes of staring up at the ceiling, she silently got a book from their bookshelf. She fell asleep reading an old book she had read many times before, one about a hero climbing a mountain and fighting a dragon with only a wooden sword. Even when Rosella was very young, she had thought the story did not sound real, not at all. You can't fight a dragon with a wooden sword, no matter how strong you are, she thought sleepily. She fell asleep face-down in the book, the candle still burning.

When Rosella woke the next morning, her neck hurt, and there was a little bit of drool stuck to a page of the book. It was the page where the hero fought ghosts in a haunted cave. He spent pages walking around in the dark. It was one of the most boring parts of the book, which may have explained why she fell asleep reading it.

From her bed, she could see through the window, and she could see that the rain had stopped. The sun was bright. The ground was still wet, but as long as the rain was gone, Rosella was happy.

Rosella jumped down from the top bunk. Her feet stung when she hit the hard wood floor, but she didn't care. The weather was nice, the trader was coming, and there was no way she was going to spend any more time inside than she had to.

Rosella dressed quickly. She considered wearing her nice shoes— which weren't really very nice—since the trader was coming that day. But the ground outside would be muddy. So, she wore her old, dirty leather boots, and dressed in thick, warm clothes, made of red and brown wool. The sun may have been out, but it was always chilly after a rain.

No one was in the house, or at least, Rosella didn't see anyone as she exited the house. Maybe the others were already waiting for the trader to arrive. That reminded her; she needed to bring money if she wanted to get anything from the trader. She ran back to her room, lifted up her mattress, and pulled out the small bag of emeralds that she had hidden away. It wasn't a lot of money, but it would do.

She opened the door, and jumped back. Grayson was standing in front of her door. He had his hand raised to knock, and he seemed just as startled as she was.

"Hi," he said. Although it was no longer raining, he had his hood pulled over his head. Maybe he was afraid it would start raining again. Grayson was her age, and although they were cousins, they looked nothing alike. Grayson was small and pale with dark, straight hair; Rosella had curly brown hair that went crazy in the summer, and was at least four inches taller than her cousin. Still, Grayson was her favorite relative. He was always willing to go on adventures, no matter how short notice. "You slept late," he said plainly.

"Not that late," she said. She yawned and rubbed the back of her hand over her eyes. "The trader isn't here yet, is he?"

"He's setting up his tent right now," Grayson said. "Are you ready to go?"

Rosella nodded. "I am. Come on."

Grayson carried his own bag of emeralds, slightly smaller than Rosella's bag. She knew what Grayson would buy; he would buy as many books as he could afford. Grayson loved books, but it was not just books. It was stories that he was obsessed with. Rosella was looking forward to finding a good bow or maybe even a new sword. Grayson, however, would be just as interested in the stories the trader had to tell them as he was in what was being sold. The trader always had some far-fetched story to tell, and Grayson was always more than willing to believe it was all true.

They chatted about what they would buy, and about the weather. Grayson told her that the Norwich farm had flooded the night before, flooding their wheat crop. They had saved some of it, but they had lost a lot.

"It's a shame," Grayson said, "Because they were going to finish harvesting the wheat this morning and sell it to the trader."

Rosella shrugged. "They'll be fine. They can sell what they have, and the village would feed them if they didn't have enough to eat. It's no big deal."

Grayson looked at her. "That's not very sympathetic, Ros."

Rosella shrugged. "It wasn't. I'm sorry. I'm just feeling sort of...bored."

"But the trader's here today," Grayson said. "That's more excitement than we usually get."

"That's my point," Rosella said. "An old man trading corn for cloth is the most exciting thing that's happened in this village for a long time."

"And that's not very exciting," Grayson said. He shrugged. "I understand, Ros. But there is not much we can do about it."

Rosella sighed. "Maybe. If I can get a new bow from the trader, I think that will be enough for today."

Grayson nodded. "I understand. It's boring here. So when something does happen, we need to take advantage of it."

"I guess you're right," Rosella said. "But that doesn't mean I like it."

"Neither do I," Grayson said. They walked in silence until the trader's tent came into view.

Chapter 2: Rozzie & Grayson Meet the Trader

Every few months, the trader would stop by the village and set up his little tent. It was a yellow and brown striped tent, the same yellow and brown striped tent that he had been using since Rosella was a small child. It was covered in patches of many different colors, and from many different kinds of cloth, but the base was still brown and yellow. It was a large tent, but not large enough to cover anything. If it was still raining, half of the things he was selling would have gotten wet.

Many different items were laid out on the wide tables that he set up. The trader, whose name was Norwich, was standing behind the table, talking to a group of villagers. Rosella didn't know if Norwich was his first name or his last name. He was a big, friendly man, although he had bad breath and usually talked too loudly.

Behind the trader was his wagon. It was huge, even taller than it was wide, and was pulled by four brown horses that were tied up behind Norwich. One was drinking water, two were eating, and one was just looking around. Rosella wanted to go say hi to the horses, but Norwich had told her that they weren't friendly. And the last thing Rosella wanted was to get bitten by a horse.

Norwich lit up when he saw Rosella and Grayson and waved them over. He had finished his talk with the adults. Rosella and Grayson walked quickly to his table.

"Hi, Norwich," Grayson said. He was already looking through the stack of leather-bound books. They came in many different sizes and shapes. Some where only forty or fifty pages thick, while one that Grayson was looking at looked like it weighed twenty pounds.

"Good morning, kids," he said. "Looking for anything in particular?"

"The usual," Grayson said. He was already reading the first few pages of one of the books. Rosella looked up and down the table. Potions, food, bags of spices and medicine. None of those things interested Rosella. She found the tools and weapons section quick enough. There were the usual assortment of bows, gardening tools, shovels and swords. She barely noticed any of those things, though. What she noticed right away was a sword. It wasn't made of stone or iron, like the few other swords that Norwich had put on the table. It was made of shining blue diamond. The sun lit it up beautifully, and Rosella was drawn to it like a moth to a flame.

Norwich noticed Rosella's interest and said, "I think that will be too expensive for you, young miss."

Rosella thought about that, and checked her small bag of rubies. She maybe had enough for an iron sword. But diamond was far, far more expensive than iron. She sighed. "You're probably right."

"Between you and me, I don't think anyone in this village will be buying it," Norwich said, leaning over to speak to her. His breath smelled like garlic and carrots, but Rosella didn't want to insult him by saying anything, so she just nodded and let him talk. "But I just found it, and I thought maybe someone would be interested."

"You found it?" Grayson asked. Rosella wanted to ask more questions about the sword—specifically, she wanted to ask if she could hold it—but Grayson's question got Norwich's attention.

"Yes I did, young sir. Found it atop Shell Mountain a few weeks back. Do you know where Shell Mountain is?"

"Of course we do," Rosella said. She wasn't sure if Grayson knew it, but she did. It was barely a mountain at all; more of a tall hill. But it was beautiful, covered in tall, green grass and pine trees. She had gone exploring around the base of the mountain many times, although she had never gone more than halfway up.

"Well," continued Norwich, "I was looking for a river—my poor horses were out of water, and I needed some myself. I ended up in the field to the west of the mountain—you know the spot."

Grayson shrugged, but Rosella knew what he was talking about. There was a huge field of red and yellow flowers to the west of the mountain. "I know it," she said. "Go on."

Norwich was a great storyteller; he knew how to surprise, he knew what parts would get the biggest reaction, and he knew how to make even boring things interesting. Grayson was hanging on his every word, but Rosella just wanted to know what happened. It was a problem she had; when she read books, she had to try very hard not to skip to the end.

But she knew better than to interrupt—that would just make the story last longer. So she bit the inside of her cheek and let Norwich talk. He told them about exploring the field, about finding a row of ants carrying a gold coin on their backs—Norwich also had a habit of telling tall tales. Sometimes she didn't know when to believe him, but he did have the diamond sword.

Eventually, Norwich had found some old stone steps. Grass and flowers had grown over them. "I'm sure I was the first person to climb them in a hundred years at least," he boasted.

Norwich was explaining, in great detail, how he had made his decision to leave his horses with the wagon, instead of trying to walk them up the stairs. That was when Rosella lost her patience. "What was at the top of the stairs?" she said as politely as she could. Grayson gave her a look, but Norwich didn't seem to mind.

"A temple, young miss," he said. "Bigger than this whole village, and crumbled to pieces." He spread his hands over the table, as if to show how massive it was. "I didn't have the time to properly explore it—my horses were waiting for me, remember—but I found this beauty inside an old wooden chest." He rested his hand on the sword's handle. Every time he moved it, it glinted in the sunlight. "Along with a pocketful of emeralds, but the sword is the real treasure."

"Why didn't you keep looking?" Rosella asked. "There must have been more treasure there, right? Why did you keep looking after finding the sword?"

"The sword and the emeralds," Norwich reminded her. Grayson laughed at that. Rosella rolled her eyes. "But no, young miss, I take your meaning. But I'm not as young as I once was. The chest was right near the entrance. I'm sure there's more treasure deeper in, but I'm in no shape for that sort of thing."

But me and Grayson are, Rosella thought. Grayson was not as strong or as fast as Rosella was, but he was quick and quiet. He was also small enough to fit through any narrow passages. They would make a good pair of treasure hunters, Rosella thought to herself. Norwich the trader had started talking about a boar that had attacked one of his horses.

Rosella thought about the ruins on top of Shell Mountain, and kept thinking about it even after she left. She bought a bow and a new pair of leather gloves, and her cousin Grayson bought a stack of books, including a journal with a silver lock on the front. Rosella asked Grayson what he was going to write about in the journal, but he wouldn't say.

Rosella lay in bed that night staring at the ceiling, still wearing her clothes from earlier in the day. She was lying on top of her blanket. She had her candle lit, but she wasn't reading anything. Instead, she was thinking about the temple on top of Shell Mountain. A lot of the time, Norwich just made things up. Or at least, Rosella thought he was making things up. She had lived in the village her whole life, and she had never traveled very far from home. She didn't know everything. Not yet, at least.

She didn't think the trader was lying. His story had a lot of details. They were the kind of details that were difficult to make up, and he described the field of flowers so well that he must have been there. Plus, he had the diamond sword. That was a big piece of proof, Rosella thought.

Chapter 3 – Grayson Hatches A Plan

The next day was bright and sunny. The only clouds in the sky were very long and thin, and never came close to blocking out the sun. Rosella woke up, ate breakfast with her family, and then immediately went to Grayson's house.

She knocked on the door, and Grayson's father—who was also Rosella's uncle—answered the door. He was yawning when he opened the door. "Oh, hi Rosella," he said. He smiled. "Excuse me. I just woke up. Colton's still eating breakfast. Come on in."

"Thanks, Uncle Roger," Rosella said. She had made a decision during the night, and she had to talk to Grayson about it. But she had to talk to him when he was alone. The plan involved an adventure, and if his parents heard, there was no way they would be able to go.

She sat at the breakfast table and waited patiently while he ate. Grayson had a lot to tell her; he had stayed up all night reading a book about a place called the Nether. He talked about the big stone portals that you could use to travel from this world to the Nether, and about all the different monsters that lived in the Nether. It was kind of interesting, Rosella thought, but it wasn't what she wanted to talk about.

When he finally finished his meal, she dragged him out by the arm. She barely gave him time to put on his boots. "Come on, I have to show you something," she lied. She couldn't let Grayson's father hear what she had to say. She didn't want to get caught, and she definitely didn't want to get caught right away. If she got in trouble right away, she would be punished before she even got to do anything fun.

"What's the hurry?" Grayson asked. He pulled his arm free from Rosella's grip.

"I've been thinking about that temple," she said.

"What temple?" Grayson asked. She couldn't believe he had forgotten already.

"The one that Norwich told us about. The one on top of Shell Mountain." She realized that her voice was a little too loud. She looked around; no one seemed to notice them. She whispered, " The place where he found the diamond sword!"

They walked near where the trader had been just the day before. Rosella could still see the wagon tracks in the mud. "Oh!" said Grayson. "I remember, yes. I've never been to Shell Mountain before, though."

"I have," Rosella said, "And I know the exact place he's talking about. I could find those stairs, easy. We could explore the temple, and who knows what kind of treasure Norwich left behind?"

Grayson didn't say anything at first. Then he smiled. "Okay. That would be fun. It would give me something to write about in my journal, at least." Then he frowned. "But there's no way our parents would let us go. Could we sneak out?" Rosella was surprised; Grayson never caused any trouble. Maybe he was just as bored as she was.

"No, we can't sneak out," Rosella said. "Shell Mountain is a full day's walk. We'd be gone for at least three days. I think they would notice."

"I think you're right," Grayson said. "Well, maybe we can get permission?"

Rosella laughed. "Do you really think our parents will let us go? There's no way they would let us go off on our own for three days."

Grayson shrugged. "Okay, you have a point. So what's your plan?"

Rosella looked up at the sun for a moment. She closed her eyes and let the sunlight warm her face. "I don't know," she said honestly. "Do you have any idea?"

Grayson thought for a moment. He folded his hands over his stomach and hmmmed very loudly. Then, after a few seconds, he said, "Yes, I do."

Grayson didn't explain his whole plan at first. At first, he just said, "Don't say anything for now. I'll get in contact with you later tonight, at dinner." Then, he walked over to the muddy tracks, and stared at them for several minutes. When Rosella asked him what he was doing, he just waved her off.

Rosella wanted to know more, but Grayson wasn't talking. So she went for a walk in the forest with her new bow and a dozen arrows. She tried to take down a few wild chickens, but she kept missing. She was too distracted to properly aim.

That night, Rosella's family ate dinner at Grayson's house. They did it once or twice a week; Rosella's mother and Grayson's mother were sisters, and they liked to get the families together as often as they could. Rosella didn't mind; it gave her a chance to have some different food. She liked her mother's cooking, but a change was always nice.

It was over dinner that Grayson hatched his plan. "I found something today," he said, when dinner was almost over and things were quiet.

"What did you find?" asked Grayson's father. He was still picking at the roasted chicken on his plate, but he seemed to be paying attention to his son.

Grayson pulled a small book from his pocket. Rosella recognized it; it was the journal that Grayson had bought from the trader the day before. The silver lock was still in place, but other than that it looked completely different. It was filthy, for one thing; it was covered in mud. Grayson held up the book so they could get a closer look at the cover.

The word "ledger" had been written on the front. "I found it where Norwich's tent was yesterday. I think he left it behind. It looks important."

"Let me see that," said Grayson's father, and Grayson handed the book to him. He inspected it for a few long seconds. The rest of the family looked on silently. Grayson's father tried to force open the book, but the little lock was tougher than it looked. It wouldn't budge. Eventually, he put the book down on the table. "Well, just as well. It must be Norwich's ledger, and that's something private." he said to himself. "You say you found this on the ground?"

Grayson nodded. "Yes, in the mud. Right near where the tent was."

"What's a ledger?" asked Rosella.

"Its a list of everything Norwich bought and sold," Grayson explained. "It is a very important tool for a trader."

"Well I'm sure Norwich wants it back," Rosella's mother said. Grayson look at Rosella, and Rosella finally figured out her cousin's plan. She stopped herself from smiling. *Very clever, cousin,* she thought. She felt a bit bad about being so sneaky, but they would be back in a few days, and there was no way their parents would ever find out. That is, if she played her cards right.

Rosella took a long sip of water and then said, "Well, is Norwich coming back soon?"

"Not for a while," Rosella's father said. "A few months, at least."

"Will he need the book before that?" Rosella asked.

Grayson's father looked thoughtful. "I would imagine so," he said. "Grayson is right, a trader needs his records."

"I'm sure he'll miss it," said Rosella's mother.

"What if he doesn't?" Rosella added. "Me and Grayson could probably catch up with him and return it. All we'd have to do is follow the road."

"Norwich *is* easy to find," Rosella's father said. He glanced over at his wife, Rosella's mother. "They would only have to follow the road, and I'm sure Norwich would be grateful. Who knows, they may even get a reward."

Rosella's mother looked suspicious. She picked up the journal. She inspected the book for a long moment. Rosella was nervous, and she imagined that Grayson was nervous as well. If Rosella's mother realized that it wasn't Norwich's book, they would both be in a lot of trouble.

Instead, she looked at Rosella and said, "Well, I suppose. I know you've been wanting to go on a trip, Rozzie. If you want to go, of course."

"I do!" Rosella said. She grabbed the ledger from her mother's hands, and passed it back to Grayson. "I mean, I do. Grayson?"

Grayson nodded. "Sure. Maybe he'll even give us a reward." Rosella grinned. *We'll get more than a reward,* she thought. *We'll get treasure.*

Unfortunately, the decision wasn't up to them, and the adults argued about it for a long time. First Grayson's mother didn't want them going. Then, Grayson's mother *did* want them to go, but Grayson's father thought the weather might be bad. Then, Rosella's mother said that she would go with them. That would have been even worse than not being allowed to go at all. However, all the adults agreed that they were far too busy to go themselves. That just left Rosella and Grayson.

In the end, though, all of the grown-ups agreed that they were old enough and that, as long as Rosella took care of Grayson, they could go. Grayson turned red when his mother said that he needed "looking after," but he did not say anything. Grayson usually didn't complain about anything, but Rosella could tell when he was embarrassed.

Still, they were allowed to go, which was all Rosella cared about. They planned for their trip that very night, as soon as dinner was over. Grayson didn't have much in the way of exploring gear, so Rosella lent him a sword and her old bow. Grayson borrowed some old leather armor and a leather helmet from his father, and Rosella borrowed twenty arrows from her mother.

"Just in case," she cautioned. "Don't go wasting them. Only use them if you need them. And if you shoot one, try to get it back?" Rosella laughed at that, even though she knew that her mother was serious. Rosella knew that making arrows took a lot longer than you would think.

Chapter 4 – The Adventure to Shell Mountain

They left early the next morning. Their entire extended family - about fifteen people in total, including a few babies and their great uncle Saxon - was there to wish them goodbye. It was a beautiful day out; Rosella could hear the ducks quacking by the pond on the other edge of town, and her younger relatives were running around on the grass instead of saying goodbye. Rosella didn't mind. That's what she would be doing if she was still six years old, after all.

They left the village walking backwards and waving to their family, promising to be back soon. It wasn't until they were a mile and a half out of the village that Rosella punched her cousin softly in the shoulder and said, "Your plan worked perfectly, cuz. Congratulations."

Grayson smiled a little bit, but then he looked worried. "I feel sort of bad about lying. *And* I ruined my new journal."

"Oh, don't be so sensitive," she said. "It's fine. We won't get in trouble, I promise. And I'll buy you a hundred new journals with all the money we find."

"But you don't even know there *is* any treasure!" Grayson said. Rosella could tell that he was getting nervous all of a sudden, now that the dangerous part was over. She was glad that he had waited until *after* they left the village to panic.

"Grayson, relax. Even if there isn't any treasure, don't you want to go on a real adventure?"

Grayson took a deep breath. "I do, I do. Sorry. I just got scared."

"It'll be fun," Rosella told her cousin. "I promise." Grayson smiled and nodded. He still looked a little nervous, but that was understandable. At least he was trying to be brave.

They walked for hours and hours that day, although they took a break every few hours to eat food and tell stories. Rosella told Grayson about the family of foxes she had seen playing in the shallow water a month earlier; Grayson told Rosella the story of how Shell Mountain got its name.

Rosella hiked a lot, and she would have been able to walk all day without stopping. Her cousin Grayson was healthy, but he didn't go out as often as Rosella did, and so she had to stop more often. She didn't mind. Grayson was actually keeping up better than she had expected. Although, from the way he was holding the bow, it was obvious that he didn't know how to use it.

By noon, they could see the very tip of the mountain over the top of the trees. According to Norwich, the temple was somewhere near the top of that mountain. From the ground, Rosella couldn't see anything, as hard as she looked. She almost tripped over a root and fell on her face, but she was able to save herself at the last second.

Rosella was so focused on the mountain ahead of her that she didn't notice the field of flowers until Grayson said something. Then she looked down, and saw that she was standing in the middle of a great wide field of flowers. They were mostly red and yellow, which made the entire field look orange if you were far enough away. Occasionally, there were little blue flowers, and Rosella saw some cotton plants as well.

"You were right, it's beautiful here," Grayson said. He reached down and plucked a red flower. He twirled the flower between his fingers and said thoughtfully, "Even if we don't find a temple, it was worth coming here."

"We're going to find the temple," Rosella repeated. Still, she didn't see the stairs anywhere. "Where did Norwich say we had to go again?"

"He didn't, really," Grayson said. "He just said it was around here somewhere."

The next hour or so wasn't a whole lot of fun. They walked up and down the meadow. It was beautiful, and it was peaceful, but it wasn't what they wanted. The walked up and down, up and down, until they found some hoofprints in the ground. The dirt was still soft and muddy from the long rain, so the impressions in the ground were deep and clear.

Once they found the hoofprints, they started to figure out where Norwich had been. Once they found his footprints in the mud, it became easy. His footprints weren't as deep as the horse's hoofprints, because of the big weight difference.

Eventually, when the sun was halfway down the sky, they found the stairs, hidden behind overgrown bushes. The way Norwich had described it, it seemed like the stairs would have been twenty feet wide. Instead, the temple steps were very narrow.

"Are you sure these are the stairs?" Grayson asked.

Rosella nodded. "I'd say so. Look." She pointed to the muddy footprints that seemed to belong to Norwich. They came up right to the steps, and there was even a muddy footprint on the first step.

Grayson wanted to take a rest before they started walking up, but Rosella was too excited. "Come on, we'll rest halfway up," she said. Grayson sighed, but nodded.

The staircase was so narrow that they had to walk up in single file. Rosella went first, and Grayson walked behind her. The staircase looked as if it had once been beautiful. But no one had taken care of it over the years. The trees and the grass had overgrown the path, and they had to duck underneath low branches. Rosella was glad that she had worn long sleeves. Otherwise, the thorns would have scratched up her arms.

As Rosella had promised, they stopped to eat lunch halfway up. It was a very late lunch, and they were both starving. They each ate half of a roasted chicken, along with a wrapped slice of cake for dessert.

It was beginning to get dark. Rosella thought about stopping for the night, but, surprisingly, Grayson said they should keep going. "Anyway," he said, "I don't want to sleep on a hill."

"Are you afraid of rolling down the mountain while you're asleep?" Rosella asked.

Grayson shrugged. "Only a little."

It was less than a half hour after that when they saw the building. At first, they couldn't quite tell what it was. They only got quick glimpses of a stone wall through the branches. Then, suddenly, they walked out into the open, and they saw the temple.

Rosella had never seen anything like it. The temple was at least five stories high, and there were tall stone towers at each corner of the building. Many of the stone towers had crumbled. The building was not in good shape, but it was still very impressive, and Rosella could tell how beautiful it would have been. The walls had been painted light blue, but most of the paint had chipped off.

They stopped outside the temple door to check their equipment. Rosella lit a torch, and she led them through the door. Grayson stayed close behind her at first, but once they were actually inside the temple, it wasn't very scary. There were no spiderwebs—and no spiders—and it was actually kind of bright. The temple had a lot of large windows with no glass in them, so plenty of light was coming in. Still, there were a lot of shadows, so Rosella kept her torch.

The inside of the building was in bad shape, but it was still the most impressive building that Rosella had ever seen. The ceilings were at least thirty feet high, and there was a big, rusty chandelier hanging above them. Along the walls, someone had carved a bunch of different markings. Rosella asked if they were writing, but Grayson said he didn't know.

After a few minutes, when Grayson felt safer, they separated. Grayson went over to take a look at the letters carved into the walls, while Rosella looked around for treasure.

It didn't take her long to find what she was looking for. There were small wooden boxes stacked in the corners of the room. Some of them were empty, and some of them were full of dirty cloth. But some of them had emeralds in them, and some even had small gold coins. They didn't look like any coin that Rosella had ever seen before; they had a picture of a dragon sitting on the island on the front, and more of the strange writing on the back. But it was still gold, which meant it was still worth a lot.

She ran over to show Grayson what she had found, but, at first, she could not find him. She looked at the carved letters that Grayson had been inspecting. She couldn't make heads or tails of them. She wondered who had written them, and, more importantly, what they said.

She looked for Grayson for a few minutes before she started to worry. "Grayson?" she called out. Her voice echoed. After a few seconds, she heard Grayson's voice come echoing back.

"I'm over here," came his voice. "Towards the west wall."

It took Rosella few seconds to remember which way was west. When she did, she jogged over, jumping over fallen stones that got in her way. Her backpack jingled as she ran. When they *did* see the trader next, she was going to buy everything he had.

She found him standing at the bottom of a ladder. It wasn't one of the wooden ladders that Rosella had seen before. It was made of stone, carved right into the wall. At the top of the ladder, she could see sunlight. "It must lead to the roof," Rosella said.

"Want to check it out?" Grayson asked. Rosella didn't answer him. Instead, she just started to climb. Grayson was right behind her.

It was a long climb up. Rosella's arms were starting to grow tired when they neared the stop, and she was pretty sure she was stronger than her younger cousin. She suddenly became worried that he would fall.

When she hadn't heard him say anything in a while, she stopped and said, "Are you okay down there?" she asked.

"I'm fine," he said. "Just keep moving. I can't climb when you stop." So, she kept climbing.

The wind was strong when they emerged onto the roof. Rosella gave Grayson a hand up; he was a little unsteady, but she wasn't sure if that was because of the height, the climb, or just the wind.

"This was worth the climb," Grayson said, catching his breath. He was right. Rosella had thought that the roof would be a mess, like the rest of the temple. Instead, it was beautiful. There was thick, green grass growing from the roof, and there was a gold and silver fence running around the edge. There was a white stone bench sitting in the middle of the grass. Even though it was made of stone, Rosella thought it looked very comfortable.

The sun was warm, and the grass was very soft beneath her feet. She yawned. She felt very, very tired all of a sudden. She looked behind her. Grayson was already laying on the grass. He looked like a cat sunning himself on a warm day. She yawned again, bigger this time. *This isn't right,* she thought. Her eyelids felt very heavy. *Something about this garden is wrong.* She tried to figure out what exactly was wrong, but she was having trouble concentrating. The last thing she remembered was lowering herself to the ground, yawning again, and falling asleep.

She dreamed of birds, and of the ocean. She dreamed that she was flying above the ocean, and that the birds were flying next to her. The sun was bright, and the sun was bright, and she felt incredible.

Chapter 5 – Awoken in a Strange Land

Rosella felt very well-rested when she awoke, although she couldn't help but notice how uncomfortable her bed felt. She reached down to pull her cover over herself, but she didn't have a blanket. She reached around, but she couldn't find it. She opened her eyes, and was immediately surprised that she wasn't in her bed.

Her back and her legs hurt, and she noticed that she was still wearing her boots, her backpack, and the rest of her things. Her heart was beating very quickly. Where was she?

She looked around. She was in a large, stone room. Her heartbeat slowed down. *Stop*, she thought. *Think, Rosella. What was the last thing you remember?* It immediately came to mind: the temple. She had been at the temple with Grayson. *Where is he?*

She looked around, and spotted Grayson. He was lying on the ground. She ran over to him, and shook his shoulder. His eyes opened immediately. "What happened?" he said. He yawned, and looked around. "Where are we?"

"I have no idea," she said. "What's the last thing you remember?"

"The temple. We climbed up that ladder, and then..." Grayson trailed off. "And then, I don't remember. Did we fall?"

Rosella shook her head. "No, we made it to the roof. Then, I don't know... you fell asleep, and then I guess I did too."

Grayson shook his head. He still looked unsteady. Rosella helped him to his feet. She noticed that he, too, still had his bag and all of his equipment. "I kind of remember that. I remember a field."

"It wasn't a field," Rosella said. "There was grass on top of the temple."

Grayson looked at her. "Are you sure? That doesn't make any sense. Why would there be grass on top of a building."

Rosella shrugged. "Maybe I dreamed it. Maybe we're still dreaming." She checked her backpack. The gems and the gold that she had found earlier was still in there. That was some good news, at least.

"I never have dreams this realistic," Grayson said. "Or this creative." Then he said, "Look at that," and pointed over her shoulder.

Rosella hadn't really gotten a good look at the room they were in. It looked a bit like the temple they had been in before, except it was even bigger, and there were no broken stones here. The building still looked old, but it was in good shape. She turned her head to look at what Grayson was pointing to.

Behind her was a large statue. It was at least three times as tall as she was. The statue was made of beautiful white stone, except for its eyes. Its eyes were shining green jewels. *Emeralds,* she thought to herself. Each eye was big enough to buy Rosella her own horse.

"How did we get here, Grayson?" she asked, and turned back to him. He had his arms crossed and was staring at the floor, thinking.

"I don't know," he said. "I don't even know where *here* is." He was tapping his foot on the ground. He seemed nervous.

"Well then, we should have a look around right?" Rosella said. "Maybe we just fell. We're probably just in a different part of the temple, or something."

"That would make sense," Grayson said, although he did not sound like he believed it. Still, he followed his older cousin around the temple.

At first, Rosella did not know where to start. The temple, or whatever it was, was very large, and very empty. There were statues along the walls, and writing on the walls, but there was no furniture, or rooms, or people. It seemed to just be one big room. So, not knowing what else to do, she turned towards where they had woken, and noticed something strange.

She walked over to the spot where they had woke up, only a few minutes earlier. In all the confusion, she had missed the white stone bench sitting on the floor. She knelt down and stared at it.

"What is it?" Grayson asked. Rosella reached out to touch the bench. The white stone felt cold and smooth.

"I saw a bench like this on the roof," she said. She could barely remember it; it felt like a far-away dream. "It might have been the same bench."

"Oh," Grayson said. "So what does that mean?"

Rosella shrugged. "I don't know. Maybe it doesn't mean anything." She gave the bench a little push, and it tipped over onto the ground. She sighed. There was nothing else even close to interesting in the spot where they had woken up. Rosella wondered how long they had been asleep for. She felt as if she had a full night's sleep. In fact, she felt like she had more energy than usual.

Maybe they had been asleep for a very, very long time. She felt scared, really scared, for the first time. What if they had been asleep for a hundred years? They would have no homes to go back to, even if they could figure out where they were.

She walked over to the first statue that she had seen, the one with the emerald eyes. She looked at the figure more closely. The statue was very well done, and had clearly been made by someone with a lot of skill.

"Hey, look at that," Grayson said. Rosella looked, and she saw two small bronze plaques on the wall next to the statue. The room was kind of dark, so she had not seen it before. She leaned over to take a look.

The first plaque was in the same strange language that they had seen earlier. The second plaque, on the other hand, was written in a language that Rosella could understand. It said "Sir Martin, Lord of the Skylands."

"What are the Skylands?" asked Grayson.

Rosella looked up at the statue again, then she looked at the plaque again. "I don't know," she said. "Maybe..."

"Maybe what?" Grayson asked.

"Come with me," Rosella said. Grayson followed her as she ran across the floor, towards the large windows. Their footsteps echoed loudly, and by the time they had reached the window, Grayson was huffing and puffing.

Rosella stepped up to the window. She had to shield her eyes against the bright light. But when her eyes adjusted to the sunlight, she saw that they were far from home.

She saw huge, floating stone islands, and each one had grass and trees. Some even had other buildings on them. Below the floating stone islands, there was only a clear blue sky. Rosella couldn't even see the ground. *The Skylands,* she thought to herself. *That's what I would have called it, too.*

"Rosella?" Grayson said. He sounded worried.

Rosella was still looking out the window. As strange as this place was, it was so peaceful, and so beautiful. "I know, Grayson. It's a lot to deal with."

"Rosella!" Grayson said again, louder this time. She turned around. Standing in the middle of the room, right where they had been standing, was a figure wearing a long white robe. She could not tell if the figure was a man or a woman; the hood on the robe was pulled up over their face. Still, the figure seemed to be staring right at them. Although she couldn't see the figure's eyes or face, so she did not really know.

"Hello?" Rosella called out. "Can you help us? Can you tell us where we are?"

The figure didn't respond. Instead, it turned away and started to slowly walk in the other direction. "Hey!" Rosella shouted out. "What are you doing here?" Then, the figure ran. "Come back here!" Rosella ran after her, and Grayson was quick behind her.

The figure was quite fast, though Grayson was faster. He ran ahead of his older cousin. Grayson had always been quick, but Rosella did not think he would run ahead of her. He had seemed even more scared than she was by everything, and she did not think that he would *want* to reach the figure first.

The hooded figure was running towards one of the large, glassless windows. As they grew closer, Rosella could see that there was a birch-wood bow on the figure's back, as well as several arrows. The feathers on the arrows were bright blue.

The hooded figure jumped through the open window. Rosella was surprised at how high the hooded figure was able to jump. It had just *hopped* up a few feet over the windowsill.

Grayson did not slow down as he came to the window. Instead, he sped up. He took a big jump, and, again, it seemed like Grayson was able to jump higher than usual. He easily cleared the top of the windowsill and dropped out of sight. Could it be something about the Skylands?

Rosella held her breath, jumped, and shot through the window like an arrow. For a moment, she felt as if she were flying. Then, she landed on dirt and grass. She looked around for a second. She saw the hooded figure ahead of her, running towards the edge of the island. Grayson was running behind her. Grayson was quick, but Rosella could see that the hooded figure was too far ahead. She didn't know if Grayson could catch up with it.

The hooded figure ran to the edge of the floating island, and jumped. Rosella slowed down a little to watch the figure jump. Where had it jumped to?

She was terrified when she saw Grayson jump as well. She shouted out to him, "Wait!" but he was already in the air. "Grayson!" She ran as quickly as she could to the edge of the cliff, and she jumped with all of her strength.

Rosella was in the air for what seemed like a very long time. She could see the island that she was jumping to. It was at least ten or fifteen feet away, and many feet down. She told herself not to look down, because she knew that it would not help. But, when she was a second away from landing, she did look down.

From where she had stood before, she had not been able to see anything below. She had assumed that they were just out in some strange part of the world, that below them there would be an ocean, or a field, or something. But instead, she saw nothing but pure, beautiful blue below her. She couldn't even see water. Below the thin carpet of clouds, all she could see was blue.

She landed with a thump. Grayson was right ahead of her, still chasing after the figure. She looked over her shoulder at where they had come. The island they had just jumped from was a lot higher than the one they were on now. *How are we going to get back up?* She thought to herself.

They kept running, and jumping. Some of the islands were closer together; some were further apart. But it seemed like they were lighter in the Skylands. *Maybe there's less gravity here,* she thought. The hooded figure had an easy time moving from island to island, as if they had been doing it their entire lives. The fact that they were having an easy time convinced Rosella that they knew something about this place. *And if they know something about this world,* Rosella thought, *then they will probably know how we can get back home.* Once more, she yelled at the fleeing figure to come back, but she was already very out of breath, and she was not able to yell very loudly.

Finally, the hooded figure came to a dead end. The only nearby island was at least twenty feet away. Even with the light air in the Skylands, Rosella did not think that the hooded figure would risk trying to jump.

Both Rosella and Grayson were panting, and so was the hooded figure. It had it's hands on it's knees, and was breathing heavily. Although she could not see the figure's face, now that they were closer, she was sure it was a girl underneath all that cloth. Rosella could see a glittering emerald ring on one finger. She took a step forward, holding out her hand.

"We're not going to hurt you," she said in a kind voice.

The girl in the robe looked at her, and for the first time, Rosella could see her face. She looked like she was about Rosella's age. She had long, blonde hair that she had put in a complicated braid. There were pieces of string, ribbon, flowers and jewels woven through her hair. She only looked at Rosella for a moment before she turned and ran, at full speed, towards the cliff.

Rosella was barely able to yell "Don't!" before the girl threw herself off of the island. She ran to the edge just in time to see the girl land safely and run off. The island she landed on was a particularly big one, and it was covered in trees. If she got into the forest, they would never find her. She turned to ask Grayson what he thought, but Grayson had already jumped. He landed safely on his feet, and was already running after the girl in the robe.

Rosella she took a few steps back, ran at full speed, and jumped.

She seemed to fall for a very long time, and she could tell when she was about halfway down that she wasn't quite close enough. She tried to turn her body so that she was a little bit closer, but it wasn't doing any good. "Grayson!" she shouted.

Grayson turned around. He had been standing on the edge of the forest, but when he saw that Rosella was in trouble, he ran right back. He reached out a hand. She was able to grab onto his arm as she fell by, although she almost pulled them both right off the island. But while Grayson was able to pull Rosella back up onto the island, the girl in the white robe was long gone.

Rosella scrambled to her feet. "Thanks, Grayson," she said. She looked back over the edge. Her stomach dropped when she thought of how close she had come to falling off. What would happen if she fell? Would she just keep falling forever? She took a step away from the edge and took a deep breath. Then, she looked over to the woods. "We lost her, didn't we?"

Grayson nodded. "I think so." Grayson looked up at the cliff they had jumped from. "And I don't think we're going to be able to get back up there."

"I don't think so, either," she said. She dropped her bag to the grass. Her legs were tingling. She felt tired, and confused, and above all, hungry. "Are you hungry?" she asked Grayson.

Grayson looked up at the sky. "I am. What time do you think it is?"

Rosella shrugged. "I have no idea, but the last meal I ate was lunch. So, that makes this dinner, right?"

Chapter 6 – A Forest in the Sky

Grayson smiled. "I guess it does." He pulled his bag off, too. Rosella chopped down a small tree to build a campfire, while Grayson prepared dinner. It was a bit windy, but Rosella still got the fire going within a few minutes, using her flint and steel. They ate, and while they ate, they talked about what they were going to do.

"Maybe we could climb back up," Grayson said. Rosella rolled her eyes.

"How would we do that? With rope?" Rosella asked.

"We could build a ladder," he said. "We *are* in a forest. If we could cut down enough trees…"

"But we don't even know if that building will get us back," Rosella said.

That made Grayson pause and take a bite of his food. He chewed it for a long time before saying, "That's a good point." He took another bite of his food. "I think we should keep moving. We need to figure out exactly where we are."

"It doesn't matter where we are," Rosella said.

Grayson looked at her. "Well, you wanted to go exploring, right?" he shrugged. "I think this is as good a time as any."

Rosella really just wanted to go home, but she supposed she didn't really have a choice. "You're right. We might as well." They finished their meal in silence, put out the fire, and ventured into the forest.

The trees were planted tightly together. In many places, they had to climb over fallen trees, and more than once, Rosella got her bow caught on the tree. They didn't see any animals, and although they knew it was in the middle of the island, it felt like the forest stretched on around them for miles.

After ten or twenty minutes, Rosella saw a small piece of white cloth. *It looks like she got her cloak caught,* Rosella thought. Rosella suddenly felt a little bad for chasing her. *She was probably scared. I'm sure she thought we were crazy.*

They could hear the wind rushing through the trees, and the chirping of birds. And there was not a cloud in the sky, which made it odd when a shadow passed overhead.

Rosella looked up. She couldn't see very well through the tree branches, but it almost looked like a large bird was circling overhead. However, it seemed to be much, much bigger than any bird she had ever seen. She stopped, and pointed up. "Do you know what that is?" she asked her cousin.

"I have no idea," Grayson said. They kept walking and, after close to an hour, they emerged on the other side of the forest.

The other side of the forest was also right on the edge of the island, and the next island was fairly close. Rosella was a bit afraid to jump again, but if she stopped jumping, she would never get to leave the island. So, she jumped to the island first, and Grayson was quick behind her.

There were dozens of islands around them, some large, some small, but they were all very close together. On the biggest island, there was another temple made of white stone. This temple, however, was even bigger than the last one; with towers that stretched so high that Rosella couldn't see the top. There were gems running along the walls, so that the entire building sparkled in the sunlight.

"I think we should go there," Grayson said. Rosella nodded.

They hopped from island to island. Now that they were used to it, it was actually very easy. Rosella felt so much lighter here, in this strange place. *The Skylands,* she thought. She still didn't really understand what was going, and she half expected to wake up at any moment.

Chapter 7 – Island Hopping

Off to the left, there was an island that was mostly a hill. On the hill, there were seven ocelots, sleeping in the sun. Grayson wanted to stay and watch them, but Rosella pulled him by the sleeve. "We should probably go while they're still asleep," Rosella said. "I bet they can jump from island to island a lot quicker than we can." Grayson nodded.

It only took them a few minutes to get to the temple. Standing right next to it, it felt like they were in front of a mountain. Looking up at the building made Rosella dizzy. She went over to the great wooden door and pounded on it with her fist. The sound was loud, and she could hear it echo. Her fist stung as she waited for a response, but no one came to the door. She knocked again, and still, nothing. She pushed on the door, and it easily swung open. She looked at Grayson and shrugged.

Not only was this temple the size of a mountain, it also looked like it had been taken care of. There were white candles on the walls, and big, colorful tapestries on the walls. There were no windows, though, and the only way in or out seemed to be the big wooden door. The room that they were in was very large, but still, it did not seem to be the entire building. *So why aren't there any other doors?* Rosella thought.

Before they got a chance to take a real look around, though, there was a great, deafening roar, as loud as five thunderclaps. The entire island seemed to shake. Through the open door, Rosella saw that same bird-like shadow moving across the other islands.

It took a few seconds for the shaking to stop and for Rosella's ears to stop ringing. "What the heck was that?" Grayson asked.

"Something big," Rosella said. The shaking had been so severe that most of the candles had gone out, and some of them had been shaken loose of the wall altogether. "I'll grab a torch," she said. She pulled open her backpack, but Grayson put an arm on her shoulder to stop her.

"Don't," he said. He pointed towards one of the walls. Behind one of the colorful tapestries on the wall there was a bright light. It lit up the entire tapestry, which showed a picture of a knight fighting a dragon with a long, diamond-tipped spear.

They walked over to it and Rosella pushed the tapestry aside. Behind it, there was a pool of light. Rosella stepped into it.

It took her eyes a little bit to adjust. Instead of many candles, there was one huge bonfire in the center of the room, surrounded by a round metal fence shin-high. The walls of the room glowed white, and the fire was so bright that it was hard to look at. It burned bright blue. And in front of the burning fire was a thin pedestal, and on the thin pedestal was a small roll of paper.

Grayson walked over to it, ran his fingers along the cover, and then opened it.

"What does it say?" Rosella asked, shielding her eyes.

"I can't tell," Grayson said. "It's too bright in here!"

"Bring it outside," she said. "We'll look at it there."

Grayson carried the piece of paper. Rosella was happy to get out of that room. "Did you notice?" Grayson asked, rubbing his eyes.

"Did I notice what?" Rosella asked.

"That fire. There was no heat to it," Grayson said.

"You're right," Rosella said. "That *was* weird. I wonder how it works." She looked over her shoulder at the tapestry. "What does the note say?"

He cleared his throat, and read aloud. "The Shrine of the Traveler welcomes all. You have been lead here by a priest or priestess of the Skylands. You are not the first people from the surface to visit the Skylands, nor will you be the last. Those who pass the trials of this temple may travel freely between the Skylands and the surface. Those that cannot pass these trials will never leave the Skylands. This is the way it is.'"

"Is that it?" Rosella asked. "There's nothing else?"

"Yes," Grayson said. "One more thing. It says 'Reach into the fire.' And it's signed, but I can't tell what the name is. It's in that weird language we saw earlier."

Rosella felt hope for the first time in a while. "So that's it? We do these trials, and we get to go home?"

"I guess," Grayson said. He sounded skeptical. He rolled up the piece of paper and handed it to his cousin.

"So, step one, reach into the fire," Rosella said. "Do you want to do it, or should I?"

"I'm not sticking my hand in fire. And you shouldn't, either," Grayson warned. "Come on. You can't just read a note and then light yourself on fire."

"Fine," Rosella said. "I'll do it myself."

"Fine," Grayson said. He crossed his arms.

She folded the note and tuck it into her back pocket. She pushed her way past the tapestry and walked back into the small room. Grayson waited outside the room, although he pushed aside the tapestry so that he could look in.

She still couldn't feel the heat from the fire. *Maybe it's not real,* she thought. *Or maybe it will melt my hand off.* She took a deep breath and, before she could think about what she was doing, she stuck her hand into the flame.

Chapter 8 – Descending into the Cave

The moment that her fingers came into contact with the flame, it disappeared. She breathed out. "See?" she said over her shoulder. "I told—"

When she turned her head, she did not see Grayson. In fact, she didn't see a door, or a tapestry, or anything. There was only the white stone wall. She turned around in a circle, looking for anything, but she could not find anything. The door was completely gone.

"Hello?" she said, and then, louder: "Grayson?"

That was when the floor fell away. The stones right below her feet just dropped. She jumped at the last moment; she could feel the stone sinking as she pushed off of it. With nowhere else to go, she hopped onto the spot where the fire had been. The stone beneath her feet wasn't even warm.

She looked around. The center of the room, where the fire had been, was still there. But the floor around it was gone. Carved into the wall were two words. One was in the strange Skylander writing. The other one was in a language she could read. It was only one word: "Fall."

Rosella wanted a chance to think about it. But, unfortunately, she had no time. She could feel the stone beneath her feet begin to shake. So, she closed her eyes and stepped off of the platform.

She fell a long way; it felt like forever. Some strange rule of the Skylands meant that she probably wouldn't get hurt when she hit the ground. At least, she thought that was how it worked. If she didn't hit anything, though, maybe she would just fall forever. The next few seconds were terrifying. Then, she hit the ground.

Even though she was lighter in the Skylands, she still hit the ground hard enough to hurt. The bottoms of her feet hurt, as did her ankles and her shins, but she was okay otherwise. She looked up. She had fallen through a hole at least a hundred feet up. *What kind of trial was that?* She thought. Then she remembered her cousin. She had to figure out a way to get back to him. And since she had no way of going back up, she knew that she had to keep moving forward. *Just keep moving forward,* she told herself. It was the only plan she had.

She looked around. It seemed that she had come out *underneath* the main island, far beneath the temple. The island she was on was small; she wouldn't even have been able to lie down on it. She made sure that she was standing right in the center of the platform; she didn't want to get blown off by the wind. Where was she supposed to go from here?

Eventually, she found what she was looking for. At the very edge of the island, there was a ladder rung. She hadn't noticed it at first; it was painted the same light blue as the sky. "Sneaky," she said quietly to herself. She leaned over and looked. There was a metal ladder leading down the side of the island, which, she could see now, was not an island; it was a very tall tower of stone. The ladder went down and down, into a big sea of clouds.

She reached out, grabbed the ladder rung, and, with a knot in her stomach, swung her leg around. Her foot found the rung after a few seconds, and she started to climb down.

She was too afraid to look down. Instead, she just stared at the wall in front of her face, and made sure that she had at least one hand and one foot on the ladder.

Rosella had to stop twice. After all of the ladder climbing that day, her hands were growing tired. When she stopped to rest, she would hook her arm through the ladder rung so that she could rest her hands. But that hurt her elbows, so eventually she would have to start climbing again. After a few minutes, she looked down. She was just coming out of the bottom of the clouds. The ladder descended into a great dark cave. She couldn't see what was below, but she also didn't have anywhere to go but down.

When she was fifteen or twenty feet above the entrance to the cave, she looped her arm around the ladder rung. She pulled off her backpack with one hand—which was fairly difficult—and reached into her bag. She grabbed a torch, and then wedged the torch into one of the higher rungs.

Lighting the torch was the most difficult part; it was hard to use a flint and steel with only one hand. But, eventually, she was able to get the torch lit. Then she pulled it from the ladder rung and dropped it into the cave.

The torch fell for a long time, and when it hit the floor below, she couldn't see much. But she *could* see that there was a solid floor below. She thought about just falling—she would probably be fine. But she still didn't like falling much, so she decided to just climb down.

It took much longer to climb down, but, eventually, she reached the floor of the cave, which was a good forty feet below the entrance. She picked up her torch and looked around. It reminded her of the room she had been in before, except for a few differences. The stone that made up the walls was made from a shiny black and purple material. Also, there was no fire burning—except for her torch—but there *was* a rolled up piece of paper sitting on a platform. She picked up the note, put her torch on the stone platform, and unrolled it. The paper was brittle and yellow, so she had to be careful as she unrolled it.

Compared to the other note, it was much shorter. There were only three words, written carefully in the middle of the page: "Find the crown."

She turned the piece of paper over, looking for more information, but she found none. What she did see, when she picked her torch back up, was a simple wooden door set into the wall of the cave. She sighed. How long did these trials last? And how many more were there? She had no idea, and whoever had created them had not given her much information.

She spent a minute or two looking around the room for some kind of clue as to what was happening. All she found were a few feathers, an arrowhead, and a bone. She didn't get too close to the bone; she decided to just leave it on the floor where it was. Other than that, though, she couldn't find anything. So, she pulled out her sword, held her torch up in front of her, and walked deeper into the cave.

The walls were made of the same shiny black stone, as was the ceiling. She ran her hand over it; it was smooth as glass. She tapped the hilt of her sword against the wall. Since it felt like glass, she thought that it would break like glass, but that was not the case. Whatever it was, it was very hard. She didn't think she'd be able to break it, even with a pickaxe. The floor was just made of normal stone, however. That was good, because she thought that the black stone would probably be slippery.

For a while, the tunnel just went straight ahead. After a while, though, the hall split off in many different directions. Some went left, some went right, and some went up, although there were no ladders. She noticed right away that there were no paths leading down. She was fine with that; she had enough of going down. She thought about trying to climb up, but the walls were too smooth. There was no way she would be able to climb up. That made her wonder why they were there at all.

Her torch hard burned down about a quarter of the way before she saw anything other than the walls, the ceiling, and the floor.

Although at first, she couldn't tell exactly what she was looking at. Even with the torchlight, all she could see was an outline, a shadow of something that was about as tall as she was. "Hello?" she whispered, but the thing gave no response. It took a few steps forward, and Rosella took a step back. "Stop where you are," she said, raising her sword. "I don't want to fight."

But the figure kept moving towards her, and she kept moving back. She noticed that whatever the figure was, it wasn't making any sound whatsoever. There wasn't even the sound of its feet on the stone. She got a sick feeling. She thought she knew what it was, and she knew it wasn't good. She stopped moving backwards for a second, so that she could see what was coming for her.

Unfortunately, it turned out that she was right. What was walking towards her, slowly but steadily, was tall, thin, and green, with coal-black eyes and no expression on its face: a creeper.

Rosella had fought creepers before, but she knew that they were especially dangerous underground. She jumped back, and the creeper, much to her dismay, moved forward. She was too close to the creature, and there wasn't much room to run. She tried to keep it away with her sword, and then with her torch, but neither worked; creepers had no fear—except for cats, strangely. But she didn't have a cat with her, and she couldn't get close enough to the creeper to hit it. She knew that if she got too close, the monster would explode.

Finally, she got a hit in, but it didn't do any good. The creeper started to charge. By the time she had turned around and started to run away, she could already hear the creeper hissing. She knew she only had about a second before it exploded, so she jumped forward. She heard a deafening bang, and there was the heat of an explosion at her back. She landed hard on the floor.

The smoke settled, and Rosella pushed herself up off the ground with a grunt. Her torch had been destroyed, but she still had her sword in hand. She looked at where the creeper had been. Its explosion had created a big hole where, just a few seconds earlier, there had been a smooth, rectangular hallway. And, much to Rosella's dismay, the floor had been blown away. Where the floor had been, she could only see the endless blue sky.

She checked herself, to make sure she had not been injured. She was dirty, and a little shaken up, but otherwise she was fine. She sat down on the edge of the crater. What was she supposed to do now?

She picked up a small pebble, and dropped it over the edge of the cliff. To her surprise, it only fell a foot before it stopped with a "clink" sound. She paused for a moment, and then picked up another pebble. She dropped that one into the hole, and it also fell a foot before stopping with a "clink" sound. She reached out a hand.

Beneath the stone, there had been a layer of thin, nearly-invisible glass. Her torch had been put out during the explosion, so she had not been able to see it earlier. She pressed down on the glass. It didn't feel very strong. But it was the only way forward, and there was no way she could jump the gap. Even if she could run fast enough before she jumped, she would only hit her head on the ceiling a second after she jumped. It had been a very long day, and the last thing she needed was a new bruise.

Still, the last thing she wanted was for the glass to break. She thought back to winters she had spent near the village. Walking on ice was always difficult, and often dangerous. One trick she had learned as a kid was to make herself as light as possible. She piled her backpack, her tools, her bow, and everything else she was carrying on the ground. Then, she pulled a length of rope from her bag, and tied up all her things to one end, using lots of double-knots. She hoped that it would hold.

She held the other end of the rope and stepped very gently onto the glass. It felt so thin and slippery beneath her feet. She lowered herself very slowly onto it. It seemed to hold her, although it did not feel very steady.

She slowly slid her feet across the glass; she was too afraid to actually take a step. She moved as slowly as she could, and tried to keep her feet far apart. She knew that if she spread out her weight, she would be less likely to break the glass. Rosella didn't weigh all that much, but the glass wasn't strong, and even though she was being very careful, she could hear it begin to crack. *I wish Grayson was here,* she thought, and not for the first time, either. Grayson was a lot smaller than her. Plus, if she had a second person, she might have been able to figure out a better plan.

The sound of cracking grew louder. She looked down, and she could see spiderweb cracks forming in the glass. She panicked a little bit when she saw that, and tried to move faster. But moving more quickly just made things worse, and the cracking grew worse. When she was within a few feet of the other side, she jumped.

Rosella let out a deep breath when she reached the other side. She looked back. The glass was covered in cracks. Some were small, but many were large. It didn't look like the glass could take much more pressure, but she still had to bring her things over. So, still holding the rope, she began to pull her things across the glass.

Her bundle of items must have been the straw that broke the camel's back, because when her bundle was about halfway there, the glass broke.

Between all her things, there was close to forty pounds worth of stuff on the other end of the rope, and Rosella almost got pulled right off the cliff. But she braced her foot against the ground and, once she had stopped sliding forward, she started pulling the bag up.

She was panting by the time she was able to pull her things up to the surface. "That wasn't so bad," she said out loud to herself, but both her legs and her arms ached, and she knew how close she had come to falling. She untied her things, put her backpack back on, strapped her tools onto her waist, and pulled out her sword. Then, on second thought, she put her sword away and pulled out her bow. If she ran into any more creepers, she wanted to be ready. So she held her bow in one hand, her torch in the other, and kept walking forward.

There were no more side-tunnels anymore. She wondered where those other tunnels and halls had gone, but it was way too late to go check. *Besides,* she thought, *these are supposed to be trials, and trials are supposed to be difficult. If I'm running into monsters, I'm probably going in the right direction.*

It was difficult to tell how long she walked for, but she had to light another torch after a while. *How big is this place, anyway?*

Rosella got her answer very soon. She didn't realize she had gotten to the end of the tunnel until she took a step forward and noticed that the walls of shiny black stone were no longer to either side of her.

The problem with big caves, she knew, was that you couldn't see all of it at once with a torch. She couldn't see the walls, or the ceiling, which meant that she had no idea how big the cavern was. *These islands aren't that big,* she though to herself. *At least, the ones I've seen haven't been that big.*

She only took a few steps into the dark room before she saw another small pillar. She was getting used to seeing them, and so she did not hesitate to walk over and pick up the roll of paper.

The second she picked it up, the room came to light. It was a big round room, and even with all the torches, she still couldn't see the ceiling. She only knew there *was* a ceiling because she couldn't see the sky. *Or maybe it's night out,* she thought. In the middle of the massive cavern, there was a stone pyramid covered in steps. At the top of the pyramid, bathed in bright white light, there was a single, shimmering crown, made of gold, silver, and jewels. She looked down at the piece of paper. There was only one word on it, written in huge letters that took up the entire page: "Run."

Rosella heard the skeletons before she saw them, but she knew the sound all too well; the groaning, the sound of rusty swords and bows. She heard a bowstring being released, and she felt the air pressure as an arrow flew by her. She decided to take the note's advice, and she ran right for the pyramid.

Usually, she wasn't very afraid of skeletons. They were stupid, and they weren't all that tough. Her mother had always said that a skeleton was just like a human, only without all the things that made humans dangerous. But there were a lot of them, too many to fight. They were coming out of tunnels and halls, pulling themselves out of holes in the ground, and even coming in from the tunnel she had just come from. They were covering the pyramid, and soon enough, the air was full of arrows.

Rosella ran and climbed as quickly as she could, taking the stairs up the pyramid three at a time. Arrows rained around her. One or two hit her, but they just grazed off of her leather armor. The pyramid wasn't that tall, but it still felt like an eternity as she ran for the top.

When she reached the top, the skeletons surrounded the pyramid on all sides. The ones with swords and spears were climbing

50

towards her, although they weren't moving all that fast. It was the skeletons with the bows she had to worry about. She was standing on top of the pyramid, which meant that they all had a good shot at her. She grabbed the crown, and as soon as she did, she felt the wind rush around her, forcing her to close her eyes.

When she opened her eyes, she stood on top of a tall, grassy hill. The sun was bright and warm. She looked around. What had happened? Another trick of the Skylands?

Chapter 9 – Back to the Skylands

She still held the crown in her hands. She held it up to the light, and it crumbled into something that looked a lot like sand. *The crown wasn't the real goal,* she thought. *The crown is just for teleporting. The whole point of it was to get me here.*

She dusted off her hands, although she realized that she was covered in dirt and dust. *I could use a bath,* she thought. *Or maybe two baths.*

She walked over to the small pedestal that was waiting for her. She picked up the piece of paper, and unrolled it. "You have done well," began the note. "But the final trial is upon you. To travel freely between the surface and the Skylands, to become a true traveler, you must travel to the First Temple." And below those words was a small sketch of a building with a curved roof and three golden pillars sticking out the top.

Rosella ripped out the picture of the First Temple and put it in her pocket. She looked along the horizon. Far away, across maybe two dozen smaller islands, she saw a white building. Since it was so small, it was difficult to see in detail. But she pulled out the picture and held it up to the horizon. She couldn't be completely sure, but she was almost positive that it was the same temple. So she ate two apples, took five big gulps of water, and started towards the First Temple.

As she traveled, jumping from one island to another, she thought about her cousin Grayson. Her cousin was smart, and he was quick, and he knew a lot, but he wasn't the toughest kid in the world. And, more than that, he just didn't have that much experience. He didn't go exploring as often as Rosella did, he didn't know how to use a sword or shoot a bow. He *did* know how to light a fire and cook food and all that, but still, she was worried. What if something happened to her? His parents would never forgive her. *Her* parents would never forgive her. And, most importantly, she would never forgive herself.

She tried to pick up the pace, to move a bit quicker so that she could get back to her cousin, but she was so tired already, and she knew there was a long way ahead of her. She could see the First Temple, and she could see the path she had to take to get to it. And that made it even more difficult, because she could *see* exactly how far she had to go.

When she was a half a mile from the temple, five or six huge, dark blue figures flew out of the temple. And even though she was very far away, now that she had a good look, she could tell that they weren't large birds. They were dragons.

She had never seen a dragon, of course. No one had. As far as she had known, they weren't even real. There were stories, of course, and drawings, and fairy tales, but no one she knew had ever actually *seen* one.

They were still very far away, so she couldn't make out details, but she could see their massive wings, their tails the size of trees, and she saw one of them breathe a big burst of fire into the air. "Dragons," she murmured to herself. It was truly amazing, but at the same time, the worst news she could have gotten. The dragons seemed to be treating the First Temple like some sort of nest. The dragons that she had seen flying out were only the beginning. In a half-hour of watching, she counted at least a dozen separate dragons. Who knew how many more were inside, and she didn't think she could fight even one, even if she had wanted to. Which she definitely did not. She had read the stories, and looked at the pictures, and heard the fairy tales, and she knew what happened to people that tried to fight dragons.

"I have to figure something out," she said to herself. The only thing was, what? Her only idea was to keep getting closer, and to get more information. *I don't really know anything, yet,* she said.

After an hour or two, she stopped to rest. She had been traveling for a very, very long time; it felt like days since she had woken up on the floor of that temple. However, the sun was still in the sky, and it was still daytime. She wondered if the sun *ever* went down in the Skylands. She wanted to sleep, but she had trouble doing that without even the shade of a tree. It was just too bright. So, she sat on the edge of a hill and looked out over the floating islands that dotted the sky.

Rosella meant to only sit down for a few minutes, but once she was off her feet, she realized just how tired she was. She kicked off her boots, and took off her helmet. She figured that, if a dragon attacked her, leather armor wouldn't do much to stop it. She sat for some time, at least an hour, watching the dragons fly through the sky, and watching the clouds slowly move with the wind. The Skylands were beautiful, Rosella knew, but also dangerous. And way too windy.

She had her eyes on the dragon almost the entire time she sat there resting, so she noticed when something changed. A few of the dragons were diving at the ground, screaming so loud that she could hear it clearly, even though she was quite far away.

She pulled her boots back on and hopped onto her feet. What was happening? The dragons were diving, and blowing fire everywhere, and roaring. *It almost looks like they're fighting something,* Rosella thought. She thought about sitting back down and just watching the fight, but she realized that this might be her only chance to get into the temple. If the dragons were in the middle of a fight, after all, they probably wouldn't notice one small human sneaking into their temple. It wasn't a great plan, but she decided that it would be good enough.

She picked up her bow and tested the bowstring. It was in good shape; she realized that she hadn't shot a single arrow while she had been in the Skylands. If she was lucky, she wouldn't have to shoot anything, but just in case, she had plenty of arrows. She thought about the blue-feathered arrows that the robed girl had carried. She wondered who, or what, that girl had been. *I guess I don't really understand this place at all,* she thought.

She checked her sword and the rest of her supplies, and then pulled her leather helmet back on. Then, Rosella took off running.

Her legs hurt even worse than they had before. *I should have never stopped,* she thought. Her legs ached with each movement, but she ran as fast as she could. She jumped from island to island. She was getting the hang of island hopping. It wasn't all that hard, actually; you just had to use the right amount of force when you jumped. *Once you learn how to give just the right push,* she thought, *it's so easy. It almost feels like flying.*

But she knew that jumping wasn't flying, and she had to remember that. If she fell, she'd never make it back home. She thought about their little village, and how eager she had been to leave it. She had to admit, parts of this adventure had been fun—although mostly it had been terrifying. She would be glad to go home and take a long, long nap in her own bed.

When she approached the First Temple, she slowed down; she didn't want to get noticed. The fight was still raging, although she still couldn't see who the dragons were fighting. She crept across one island and, when she didn't see any dragons looking in her direction, she jumped to the next island. There usually wasn't much to hide behind on these islands, but she could always find a tree or a rock to hide behind. Once on the island, she laid on her stomach and crawled through a field of tall grass. It was uncomfortable and itchy, but being uncomfortable and itchy was much better than getting into a fight with a dragon.

Finally, she reached the First Temple. It was bigger than the other two temples she had seen put together, although it was much more plain. The other temples were covered in shining jewels and beautiful art. From the outside, at least, the First Temple was almost completely plain, without any decorations at all. *And if there are dragons living in the temple,* Rosella thought, *I can't imagine that it's very nice inside.* Still, this is where the directions had told her to come. And even if she didn't quite understand these trials, they were her only way back home.

She crept along the outer wall of the temple, with her back pressed against the smooth white stone. Whenever a dragon flew near that side of the temple, she would freeze in place, closer her eyes, and wait for it to leave. Every time, she was afraid that the dragon would notice her and dive at her, but it never happened. *They must be busy,* she thought.

She crept along the wall, looking for a way in, but she couldn't find one. *There aren't any doors on this side of the temple,* she thought with dismay. *There must be a front door. Just like the other temples.* She started creeping towards the front of the building, where the fighting was going on. She really didn't want to get any closer to the fighting than she had to, but time was of the essence. If the fighting stopped and the dragons returned to their home, she would be in a lot of trouble. She had to act right away.

When she reached the edge of the palace, she poked her head around the corner. It was hard to tell exactly what was going on; the figures were moving very quickly, both the dragons and the robed figures. Rosella realized immediately that they looked to be wearing the same robe that the girl had been wearing earlier.

There were many more robed figures than there were dragons, but it still looked like the dragons were winning. The robed figures fought the dragons with long spears, as well as arrows. She saw the blue-feathered arrows flying through the air and hitting the dragons. Some arrows did pierce the dragons, but most of them just bounced off the dragon's thick armor.

It looked as if the fight was coming to an end, though. The robed figures were falling back, running away. Only a few of them were fighting the dragons now, and it just looked like they were trying to protect their friends. Rosella figured that she had less than a minute to get through the front door of the temple before the dragons went home. From there, she only hoped that she was able to find the portal home before one of the dragons found her.

So she went around the corner as quick as she could, trying her best to stay quiet. Although, the dragons were making so much noise, she doubted that they would have noticed.

She got to the door within a few seconds. It was another big door, one that seemed almost too big for her to open on her own. But when she grabbed the huge, brass ring and pulled, the door pulled over easily. She didn't know if that was magic, or if it was just a very expensive door. And although the door didn't make a squeak, one of the dragons must have been looking in her direction, because it came barreling toward her.

Rosella only had the door a few inches open before the dragon slammed into the door, forcing it closed with a big bang. The wood beams splintered, and the ring was pulled out of her hand. She turned her head to look at the dragon, and she saw it staring back at her. Then, the dragon, which was the size of a whale and had claws bigger than her arm, breathed in. And she knew what happened when a dragon breathed out. She jumped and rolled out of the way.

She felt the heat of the fire on her back, and she was pretty sure that some of her hair had been singed, but she escaped unharmed. She popped up onto her feet. The dragon that had just tried to breathe fire on her had turned its attention back to one of the robed figured. "Run!" shouted the figure, and pointed in the direction that the other robed figures were heading.

Rosella nodded dumbly and, without looking back, ran in the direction of the robed figures. She could still feel the dragons behind her, but she did not dare to look back. She just jumped from island to island, following the long line of people ahead of her.

Chapter 10 – The Sky People

When the First Temple was out of sight, the robed figures slowed down, and finally stopped on a large, round island with dark green grass and yellow flowers. The figures pulled off their hoods. *Finally,* Rosella thought.

She didn't know what she had expected the Sky people to look like, but they just looked like normal humans to her. Most of them had dark hair, although some of them were blonde, and she saw one kid with curly, dark red hair. Just like the girl she had seen earlier, the other Sky people had jewels, ribbon, and other things woven through their hair. The older men even had decorations woven into their beards and mustaches.

From the crowd of people, a young man emerged. He was maybe ten years older than she was, and several inches taller. She tried not to blush when he walked up to her and gently took her hands. "You must be lost," he said in a gentle voice. "You're not from here."

"I'm not," she said. He let go of her hands, and she coughed nervously. "I'm from the, um. The surface."

He nodded, as if he already knew that. "You are very far from home, then. Come with us."

"Where do you want me to go?" she said.

"To our village," he said. She saw a few people in the crowd nod in agreement.

"We can't leave a surface child out here. You'd die in an hour!" said one older woman. A few people in the crowd laughed, and Rosella blushed.

"I've been here for, well, a while. And I've survived just fine," she said. "I even passed all those stupid trials."

"Did you?" asked the handsome young man.

She nodded. "I even got that stupid crown. Until it turned to dust. But now I need to get into that building to finish."

"Without your cousin?" the young man asked.

"No, of course not without—" she paused. "Wait. How did you know about him?"

He laughed. "Come with us. Grayson has been waiting for you."

The trip back to the Sky people's village was challenging. There were many steep jumps, and more than once, she had to jump down blind, falling through a hole and just trusting that there was land below. Rosella felt like she was pretty good at island jumping, but she saw now that she was still a beginner. More than once, she needed help from one of the Skylanders. They were even slowing down their pace so that she could keep up. It was very embarrassing, and it made her feel like a child, but it was better than falling.

It was difficult to tell how much time had passed, especially when the sun never set, but she thought they had traveled for at least three hours before they reached the village. Rosella has expected a few tree houses or tents, but the Skylander's village was actually much bigger than her own, and the buildings were much taller.

When she asked why the buildings were so tall, the young man, whose name was Luther, explained that they had no choice. "We can't just keep chopping down trees and growing the village, like you surface people do," he said. "You can only build to the edge of the island. So when we ran out of room, we had to build up. Still, the village is very crowded. We want to spread out to other islands."

"Why don't you?" Rosella asked.

"Because of the dragons," Luther said. "That's why we were trying to get them out of the First Temple. If we can take back the temple, we can take control of the Skylands once again. We can flourish again. We can be more than just one tiny, cramped village; we can be a nation."

She jumped over to the island. Luther had been right; the buildings were built right to the edge of the island. Most of the buildings were very thin and very tall, with narrow windows made out of colored glass. "Many of these houses only have one room on each floor," Luther told her.

"Doesn't that get annoying?" she asked. "Having to go up and down stairs every time you want to go to a different room?"

"It does," Luther admitted. "But it's not so bad."

"It would be easier living in this village if you could fly," she said, and Luther laughed.

"*Everything* would be easier if you could fly," he said. She had to agree with that.

They walked through the village, which was so tightly packed that it seemed more like a city to Rosella. There were ladders running along the sides of buildings, and she saw a lot of people climbing up and down. There were baskets hanging on long ropes. Instead of carrying things up and down, they would raise and lower things in the baskets. That made sense to Rosella; she knew how difficult it was to climb a ladder while carrying something. She wished she had

a basket and a rope when she was climbing down that ladder during the trials.

"Where's Grayson?" Rosella asked.

"He's at the town hall, with the mayor," Luther said. "We found him out near the Temple of Trials."

She was glad that Grayson was safe, but she was also feeling very guilty about leaving him. True, it had not been on purpose, but Grayson had told her not to do the trails. If she had waited, maybe the Sky people would have just found her. She could have been relaxing with Grayson, instead of fighting monsters and climbing through caves. "We got separated," was all she said.

"He told us," Luther said. Then, all of a sudden, he asked, "Did you really go through the trials?"

"I did," she said. "Although now I'm realizing I probably didn't have to."

"On the contrary," Luther said. "Without the trials, the final door will not open. And if the final door will not open, then you will never go home. If you didn't do it then, you would have had to do it now."

That made her feel better about her choice, until Luther said, "Of course, if you had come here first, we could have helped you quite a bit. Rosella sighed. *You win some, you lose some,* she thought sourly.

They walked up to a gap between the buildings. It was a big grassy patch of land that had been turned into some sort of park. Although the park was small, there were many people in it. In the center of the park was a small fountain, and on top of the fountain was a small statue of a man holding a sword. The sword was made

entirely out of emeralds. Rosella thought that it was strange that a village with so much money could be so crowded. There were emeralds and gold everywhere. Of course, neither emeralds nor gold would do any good against the dragons.

In the park, she saw a group of soldiers fighting. They wore white robes, just like the rest of the Skylanders, but they also wore steel helmets underneath their hoods. They practiced with long wooden poles, so that they did not injure each other, but their sharp steel spears were stuck into the ground beside them. Most of the people training were full-grown adults, but some of them were no older then Rosella. They practiced the same moves over and over, and after watching for a little bit, she figured out that they were training to fight dragons; they were stabbing up very high, higher than any human was tall.

Next to the spear soldiers, there were several archers lined up, firing their bows at a few straw targets. Most of the archers were her age, or younger. It seemed like the entire village, young and old, trained to fight dragons.

"Come this way," Luther said, motioning to a tall building made out of simple brick that sat on the other side of the park. Each story of the building was a slightly different color, as if they had been built at different times. Rosella realized that was probably it; long ago, it had been a small building with only one story. Each story had probably been added individually. Near the bottom, the bricks were pale and flaking, while at the top, they were deep red and looked new.

"Will they just keep adding floors to that building?" Rosella asked.

"If we take our lands back from the dragons," he said, "Then maybe we won't have to."

Rosella thought about that as Luther guided her towards the brick building, which she thought was the town hall. There was more of that strange, Skylander writing along the walls. She wondered if her journey would have been made easier if she could have read those words. The writing that she had seen in the temple on Shell Mountain had probably been warnings, telling them not to go to the roof.

The doors swung in, and Luther led her up the stairs to the very top floor. After all she had been through that day, she was exhausted, and she had to lean heavily on the railing in the stairwell. Luther was nice enough to wait for her, and eventually, they reached the top.

At the top of the stairs was a single iron door. Luther flipped a switch, and the door swung open. Through the doorway, Rosella saw her younger cousin. He was wearing one of the Skylander's white cloaks and, although he looked tired and scared, he didn't seem to be hurt. When he looked up and saw Rosella, his jaw dropped, and he ran to her, nearly tripping over his robe as he ran. "Rosella!" he shouted, and crushed her in a hug. She hugged back, with what strength she had left.

"I'm so glad you're okay," she said. "I'm sorry. I should have never gone on."

"You're right, you should have listened to me," he said. He smiled at her and said "But that's okay. I'm just happy you made it back here in one piece."

"Only barely," she said. "I could use some sleep. And some water. And maybe one of those robes."

"We can help you out with all of those," Luther said. She had forgotten that he was standing behind her.

"And then," Rosella said, "We're going to the First Temple."

Grayson gave her a look. She briefly explained about the trials, and about the First Temple, and how it had become a nest for dragons.

"Which is why we were there," Luther said.

"To drive off the dragons?" Grayson asked.

Luther nodded. "We were trying to drive the dragons from the temple, and tomorrow, we will try again. We weakened them today, and with some fresh troops, perhaps we can defeat them tomorrow."

"We're coming with you," Rosella said.

Grayson looked shocked. "Isn't that incredibly dangerous? Even more dangerous than sticking your hand in a fire?"

"Well I was fine last time," she said. "Besides, this is the only way to get home. You do want to go home, don't you?"

She was surprised to see that Grayson actually took a moment to think about that. But eventually, he said, "I guess so. I kind of wanted to stay longer. This place is fascinating. I didn't even get a chance to visit their library. But, you're probably right. It's time to go home."

"I'm *definitely* right," Rosella said. "And we may not get another opportunity at this."

Luther nodded. "Anyone that wants to can come with us, but they must fight. You can come, surface dwellers, but only if you fight."

Rosella rested a hand on her bow. "Don't worry about it. I'll join your archers. Grayson will too." She could see Grayson was about to object—he was a terrible shot with a bow and he knew it—but she stared at him with a warning look on her face, so he said nothing.

The Sky people's village was very cramped, that was true, but they were still able to give Rosella and Grayson a place to sleep that night, as well as new clothes and new weapons. Rosella changed into one of the white robes, which were comfortable, even if they did look a little silly. She kept her old boots. Even if they were uncomfortable and ugly, she was used to running in them, and she would probably have to do a lot of running on the next day.

It was always daytime in the Skylands, but the windows on her small bedroom had shudders, and her bed, although a little narrow, was comfortable. Although even if it hadn't been comfortable, Rosella was so tired that she could have slept on the worst mattress in the world. She fell asleep within a minute of lying down.

Rosella dreamed of flying again. The dream started off the same, with her soaring through the skies with the birds around her. But after a few minutes, the dream changed. Whatever was making her fly grew weaker. At first she just slowed down. Then she began sinking down, and then, falling. She woke with a start when she hit the ocean below.

She had no idea what time it was when she woke, but the knocking on her door told her that it was time to go. She dressed quickly. She left her backpack behind, and she had told Grayson to do the same. "We need to carry as little as possible," she said. "Besides, if we make it in, we won't need more than our weapons. If we don't—"

"—Then nothing in our bags will help us," Grayson said. He looked very grim. They both pulled their hoods on and headed down to the park, where the Skylander forces were gathering. There were at least a hundred of them filling the park. As soon as they arrived, the soldiers began to leave without saying a word. Rosella and Grayson followed. Rosella was curious as to why there had been no speech, but then she realized why that was. There was no speech because they did this so often, so it wasn't any kind of special event. She hoped that all their experience paid off.

Chapter 11 – The Final Battle

Rosella and Grayson were in the back of the long line. They traveled the same path they had taken the day before. Along the way, Rosella could see broken arrows and spears along the ground, left over from the previous day's battle. At first, they were silent, but as they came closer and closer to the First Temple, they grew louder, chanting in a strange language that neither Rosella nor Grayson recognized. When the First Temple came into view, they were practically screaming, and it was getting the attention of the dragons.

The blue dragons came streaming out of the temple. They had broken a giant hole in the roof, and they had also ripped the doors from their hinges. They didn't seem to have any plan, really; it seemed like they just enjoyed destroying the temple, and attacking anyone that came close. And at that moment, they were diving towards the Skylanders like hungry birds.

Since Rosella and Grayson were at the back of the line, they couldn't see exactly what was happening. By the time they reached the floating island, the battle was already in full effect. It seemed that Luther was right: their attack from the other day *had* weakened the dragons. Whereas there had been at least twenty the day before, now there was only about half that number. And while ten dragons was nothing to scoff at, it certainly made their odds a little better.

"Stop staring and shoot!" Shouted Luther. Rosella did as she was told. She pulled out one of her mother's white-feathered arrows, pulled back, aimed, and let her first arrow fly.

Her first arrow missed, as did her second, and her third, and Grayson was hardly doing any better. It turned out that the dragons knew that the arrows were coming, and they knew to dodge out of the way before they hit. And as huge as they were, they could move incredibly fast. It was just too difficult to hit them.

The Skylanders seemed to be better at it than Rosella was, but even they had trouble getting in any hits. The spearmen stood in front of them, trying to distract the dragons and stop them from getting to the archers, but more than once Rosella had to duck out of the way as a dragon flew by a few inches above her head. Once, one of the dragons grabbed at her with its claws, but she was able to twist out of the way.

The Skylanders had taken down two dragons, but there were still many left, and the soldiers were tiring. Two of the larger blue dragons had cornered about twenty of the archers. The spearmen were trying to rescue them, but it was almost impossible to sneak up on the dragons. They were too smart, and too quick, and, most importantly, they could fly. As she watched the fight, she realized that, in the Skylands, at least, flight was the ultimate weapon.

But birds and dragons aren't the only things that fly, she thought. *Arrows fly too.* She took aim again, and this time, she waited for as long as she could before she let go; she wanted to make sure her shot was perfect, and she didn't want to waste any more arrows.

When the right moment came, she released. She hit a flying dragon right in the soft spot on its belly, causing it to scream in pain and fly off in the opposite direction. She pulled out another arrow, took aim again, and fired at a second dragon. Unfortunately, while the second shot hit, it didn't seem to hurt the dragon much. All it seemed to do was draw the focus of the dragon to Rosella.

She tried to pull out another arrow, but the dragon was too quick. It clawed out at her, and while she was able to pull back quick enough to keep herself from being cut in half, the dragon's massive claws cut her bow into useless scraps. The dragon roared at her; the sound was so loud that she could feel herself being pushed back by the force of it. She drew her sword, but the dragon clawed that out of her hands as well.

"Duck!" she heard, and she did. At least a dozen archers stood behind her, and the moment she ducked, they let their arrows fly right at the monster's face. Rosella didn't see any of the arrows hit, but she *did* hear the dragon scream in pain. She didn't have time to look, though. She was weaponless, and the battle was not even close to over.

She heard a scream, and she knew immediately that it was Grayson. She turned, and saw that he had been cornered by one of the dragons. It was one of the smaller ones, but even the smaller ones were dangerous. In fact, they could be even more dangerous; they were quicker, and more difficult to hit with arrows.

Grayson was running back and forth, trying to shake the beast, but it wasn't working. The dragon was watching him like a cat watching a mouse. "Grayson! Over here!" she shouted as she picked a rock up off the ground. She hurled it at the dragon. It bounced harmlessly off its back, but it drew the beast's attention away from Grayson, if only for a second or two.

That was all the time Grayson needed. Quick as always, Grayson ran right under the dragon. "Let's go!" he shouted as he ran by her. She was quick behind him.

"We're done here," Rosella shouted to her cousin.

He shouted back, "I agree. I've had enough adventure for a lifetime. But what about them?" He motioned to the Skylanders.

She looked at them. They seemed to be winning; there were only a few dragons left, and those were growing weak. "They'll be fine, they're almost done," Rosella said. "Besides, we don't even have any weapons."

Grayson nodded. They ran right through the big hole in the wall of the temple where doors used to be. They expected another massive building full of gold and art, but instead, they found a series of dark, narrow hallways with low ceilings. They paused at the entrance.

"This doesn't look like a temple," Grayson said.

"You're right," Rosella said. "It looks like a tomb."

"What's a tomb?" Grayson asked.

"It's a building full of graves."

Grayson shrugged. "Graves are better than dragons. Come on. I want to go home."

Rosella smiled. "Okay. After you, cousin."

Unlike the earlier tunnels that Rosella had gone through, this one had no turns, no twists, no hallways. It just went forward. That was fine, as far as Rosella was concerned. It just meant that they couldn't get lost.

Except, when she heard a dragon's roar echoing down the hall behind them, and then again, closer, she realized that it also meant there was no way to escape. "Run," she said to Grayson. Then, when the screaming came closer yet again, much closer, she shouted it. "Run! Run!" And Grayson ran.

They both ran fast, but the dragon got closer and closer. Rosella kept peeking over her shoulder, and after a minute or two, the dragon came into view. It was one of the small dragons, but even then, it was barely able to fit into the tunnel. There wasn't nearly enough room to fly, so it was crawling after them with its long, vicious claws.

She looked forward again, and Grayson was gone. She was about to shout out to him when she fell. The hallway, which had seemed like it would stretch on forever, had suddenly come to an end, and the both of them fell out the bottom of the island. Then, before she even had a chance to get used to the idea of falling, she hit the water.

She desperately paddled towards the surface. She was nearly out of air by the time she reached it, and, even before she wiped the water from her eyes, she could hear Grayson panting and coughing. She opened her eyes and looked around. They were in the water— in the ocean. Had they fallen all the way from the island? She looked up, but there was nothing above them.

"Where are we?" Grayson asked. He was doggie paddling in place. He looked very confused, which was no surprise, Rosella was confused as well. She took a look around, though, and immediately she saw the shoreline. And, behind the shoreline, and through a forest, she saw Shell Mountain rising above the treetops. Even though she knew exactly where that temple was, she still couldn't see it. She wondered if it was there at all. Maybe it had been an illusion.

"We're at Trundle Beach," she said. "I've been here before." She started swimming towards the shore, and Grayson was right behind. They were only a few hours away from their village; they would be there by suppertime, if all went well!

She had more than a few new stories to tell, although the only proof that they had were the long white robes that they still wore. When they reached the shore, they laid on the beach for a while to let themselves dry off in the bright sunlight.

Rosella had nearly fallen asleep in the sun when she heard Grayson ask a question. "Do you think we'll be in trouble?"

Rosella laughed a tired laugh. "Grayson, I almost got eaten by a dragon. More than once. I don't care if my mom yells at me."

"Still," Grayson said, "I'm not sure I'm in a huge rush to get home."

Rosella nodded, her eyes still closed. "Sure. We'll take the long way back. Maybe find some treasure that we actually get to keep."

Made in the USA
San Bernardino, CA
07 July 2014